The Words of Gad the Seer

*Prophecies and Visions of
Divine Guidance*

A Modern Translation

Adapted for the Contemporary Reader

Gad the Seer
(Prophet of King David)

Translated by Tim Zengerink

© **Copyright 2025**
All rights reserved.

It is not legal to reproduce, duplicate, or transmit any part of this document in either electronic means or in printed format. Recording of this publication is strictly prohibited and any storage of this document is not allowed unless with written permission from the publisher except for the use of brief quotations in a book review.

This book contains works of fiction. Any resemblance to persons living or dead, or places, events, or locations is purely coincidental.

Table Of Contents

Preface - Message to the Reader 1

Introduction 5

The Words of Gad the Seer 11

Thank You for Reading 18

Preface - Message to the Reader

What If You Could Help Rebuild the Greatest Library in Human History?

Thousands of years ago, the Library of Alexandria stood as the crown jewel of human achievement — a sanctuary where the collected wisdom of every known civilization was gathered, preserved, and shared freely.

And then, it was lost.

Through fire, conquest, and the slow erosion of time, humanity lost not just books — but ideas, dreams, discoveries, and stories that could have changed the world forever.

Today, the Library of Alexandria lives again — and you are invited to be a part of its restoration.

Our mission is simple yet profound:

To rebuild the greatest library the world has ever known, and to translate all timeless works into every language and dialect, so that no seeker of knowledge is ever left behind again.

By joining our movement to rebuild the modern Library of Alexandria, you become part of an unprecedented mission:

- **Unlimited Access to the Greatest Audiobooks & eBooks Ever Written:**

    Instantly explore thousands of legendary works—Plato, Shakespeare, Jane Austen, Leo Tolstoy, and countless more. All instantly available to read or listen, placing a complete literary universe at your fingertips.

- **Beautiful Paperback & Deluxe Editions at Printing Cost**

    Own any title as an elegant paperback, deluxe hardcover, or stunning collectible boxset—offered to you at true printing cost, delivered straight to your door. Build your personal Library of Alexandria, crafted for beauty, built for durability, and worthy of proud display.

- **Fresh Translations for Modern Readers—in Every Language & Dialect**

    Enjoy timeless masterpieces reimagined in clear, contemporary language—no more outdated phrases or obscure references. Alongside the original versions, we're tirelessly translating these classics into every language and dialect imaginable, ensuring accessibility and understanding across cultures and generations.

- **Join a Global Renaissance of Literature & Knowledge**

    You directly support expanding our library, publishing deluxe editions at true cost, translating works into all global languages, and bringing humanity's greatest stories to people everywhere. By joining today, you're not just preserving a legacy of masterpieces; you set in motion a powerful wave of literary accessibility.

Become a Torchbearer of Knowledge.

Join us for free now at **LibraryofAlexandria.com**

Together, we will ensure that the light of human wisdom never fades again.

With gratitude and a shared love of knowledge,

The Modern Library of Alexandria Team

Visit:

www.libraryofalexandria.com

Or scan the code below:

Introduction

A Forgotten Prophet and a Recovered Revelation

The Words of Gad the Seer offers modern readers a rare and compelling glimpse into the spiritual world of ancient Israel through the voice of one of its most enigmatic prophetic figures. Mentioned briefly in the Hebrew Bible as a prophet and advisor to King David, Gad appears in the historical record as a trusted intermediary between God and the king. He is described as a man of vision, discernment, and moral authority—one whose words carried weight in the spiritual and political life of the nation. Though his contributions are only briefly cited in canonical scripture, this preserved apocryphal text expands his legacy and presents a deeper record of his revelations, visions, and prophecies.

What distinguishes The Words of Gad the Seer from other prophetic writings is its powerful fusion of visionary experiences and ethical instruction. In these pages, we find a prophet unafraid to confront kings, warn nations, and unveil the eternal tensions between mercy and justice, righteousness and corruption, the temporal and the divine. The book offers a sustained meditation on Israel's covenant with God, the spiritual responsibilities of its leaders, and the cosmic stakes of human choices. Gad does not speak merely of the past—his voice resonates into the future, addressing timeless questions of divine sovereignty, human agency, and the ever-unfolding consequences of disobedience and repentance.

The historical context of Gad's ministry is essential to understanding his message. He served during the reign of King David, a period of great transition and consolidation in Israel's history. David was a complex figure—warrior, poet, ruler, and sinner—and Gad's role as prophet was not to flatter the king but to confront him with truth. It was Gad who delivered divine rebuke after David's unlawful census, offering the king a choice of judgment and reminding him of the weight of his actions. Yet Gad also served as a channel of divine mercy, communicating hope and reassurance in times of crisis. In this dual capacity, he exemplifies the prophetic tradition at its finest: holding power to account while also holding forth the promises of redemption.

The Words of Gad the Seer combines autobiographical reflection with divine revelation. We hear the prophet's own voice—his doubts, fears, and moments of awe—as he receives visions from the Most

High. These are not abstract dreams but vivid encounters with spiritual realities. Gad is shown the heavenly temple, the workings of angelic orders, and the fates of nations. He is taken beyond the veil of the visible to witness the forces that govern the destiny of Israel and the world. In these visions, the reader is drawn into a cosmic perspective that frames earthly events within a divine narrative. The wars of kings, the sins of rulers, the sufferings of the people—all are seen not as isolated tragedies but as elements in a larger spiritual drama.

Divine Justice, Covenant Faithfulness, and Spiritual Renewal

One of the central themes of The Words of Gad the Seer is the relationship between divine justice and covenant faithfulness. Gad's prophecies emphasize that God is not indifferent to injustice, idolatry, or rebellion. When the people turn from the covenant, judgment follows. Yet that judgment is always tempered by mercy, and repentance opens the path to restoration. The message is consistent: the God of Israel is both holy and compassionate, demanding righteousness while offering forgiveness. The prophetic role, as exemplified by Gad, is to call the people back—to awaken them to the presence of God in their midst and the urgency of obedience.

Gad's insights into the spiritual dimensions of leadership are particularly powerful. He addresses not only the king but also the people, reminding them that national destiny is tied to collective morality. Leaders are accountable for their actions, and their private sins have public consequences. But the people, too, bear responsibility—to uphold justice, resist idolatry, and honor the covenant. In this way, The Words of Gad the Seer functions as a manual of spiritual leadership, offering timeless principles for anyone entrusted with authority.

The text is also deeply mystical. Gad speaks of heavenly realms, angelic hosts, and divine mysteries that echo the visionary traditions of Enoch, Ezekiel, and later apocalyptic literature. He reveals a multi-layered universe in which every earthly action has cosmic significance. The fate of Israel is tied not only to human history but to spiritual forces beyond sight. This worldview challenges modern readers to consider the spiritual consequences of moral choices and the unseen dimensions of divine interaction.

At the same time, Gad's message is intensely personal. He does not only speak of nations and kings—he speaks to the heart of the individual. He warns against pride, encourages humility, and teaches that God desires not ritual alone but sincerity, compassion, and faithfulness. He invites each reader to examine their own life in light of divine truth, to seek forgiveness where they have erred, and to walk in righteousness. His words are not only for his generation—they are for all who would hear the voice of a prophet calling across time.

This modern translation of The Words of Gad the Seer has been prepared with great care and reverence. Archaic phrasing has been clarified, the poetic structure preserved, and theological depth rendered in accessible language. The goal has been to retain the majesty, urgency, and inspiration of the original while making its profound teachings available to contemporary readers. In doing so, this adaptation seeks not only to inform but to transform—to stir the soul, awaken the conscience, and call each reader into deeper relationship with the God who speaks through His prophets.

To read this text is to step into sacred history. It is to stand beside a prophet who heard the voice of God and dared to speak it. It is to witness the spiritual foundation of a nation and the eternal truths that still guide those who seek justice, mercy, and humility. Let The Words of Gad the Seer lead you not only into the past, but into your own soul—into reflection, repentance, and renewal. May its visions open your eyes, its wisdom challenge your heart, and its message guide

Translated by Tim Zengerink

your steps on the path of righteousness.

The Words of Gad the Seer

Discovered in India in 1786 by Scholar J. G. Eichhorn at a synagogue of Cochin Jews

In the thirty-first year of King David's reign in Jerusalem, which was also his thirty-eighth year as ruler, God spoke to Gad the Seer in the second month near the Kidron stream. God told him, "Get ready and stand in the middle of the stream. Shout loudly, 'Wait and prepare! Wait and prepare! Wait and prepare!' because a vision is coming for the son of Jesse."

God also told Gad to turn east toward the city, lift his hands to the sky, and speak these words. Gad obeyed.

When he finished, he opened his eyes and saw a vision. In front of him was a yoke of oxen, led by a donkey on one side and a camel on the other. Then, a loud voice like thunder called out in a sorrowful tone, "Seer! Seer! Seer! These four things have confused God's people.

"The pure and impure have been mixed together, but impurity is now stronger. A foreign power has risen over them, controlling the righteous and betraying them. It tries to destroy holiness, lift up wickedness, and disguise impurity as if it were pure."

After the voice spoke, a strong shaking caused impurity to tremble. A powerful wind swept the donkey and the camel into the moon. The moon opened like a glowing half-circle stretching to the ground.

Then, a figure came down from heaven. It was the Son, appearing as a man with a crown on His head. Over His right shoulder, He carried a lamb that had been rejected and despised. On His crown were three shepherds, bound with twelve chains made of gold and covered in silver. The chains sparkled as the lamb's voice roared like a lion. The lamb cried out, "Woe to me! Woe to me! Woe to me! My image has been ruined, my refuge is gone, and my enemies have taken everything from me. I have been defiled until evening."

Then, a man dressed in linen appeared, holding three vine branches and twelve palm branches. He walked up to the Son, took the lamb from Him, and placed the crown on the lamb's head. He laid the vine and palm branches on the lamb's heart. Then, he cried out in a voice as loud as a ram's horn, saying, "This impurity, and the one who carries it, have forced their way into what was meant to be pure. But my covenant remains with the vine branches and the palms."

The Son, who shepherded the lamb, declared, "With me, only purity has a place—there is no room for impurity. I am the Holy God, and I will not accept anything unclean. I created both the pure and the impure, and I see them both. But purity is greater, just as a man is greater than his shadow. A shadow exists because of the man, just as impurity only exists because purity was first. But purity is meant to bring peace, whether for the pure or impure, and this truth will never change.

"The doors of wisdom have been shut since the eight vine branches died. This is written in the true book of righteousness. But because the people have wandered and been divided, understanding has been hidden—until the time when I act in power to bring favor."

In the vision, Gad saw impurity being cast out of the moon. It was handed over to judgment, crushed into dust, and scattered by the wind. The day burned like a furnace, wiping away impurity and sins. The lamb was placed upon the Son, sealing a covenant forever.

Then, the lamb took the peace offerings—the sacrifices that had been mixed with impurity—and brought them to the altar before El Shaddai, the Mighty Lord of Hosts. It was a powerful and sacred moment as the lamb approached the holy place with deep reverence. As I watched, I heard the lamb begin to sing, lifting its voice in worship and gratitude.

Translated by Tim Zengerink

The lamb sang, "I will praise You, O Yahweh! Though Your anger was fierce against me, You have shown me mercy. Yahweh is my strength, my song, and my salvation. He is my redeemer and deliverer. I will sing to Yahweh, for He is exalted above all. He has thrown the horse and its rider into the depths of the sea.

Rise up, Wisdom, and glorify the Lord! Rise up, Power, and honor Him! Rise up, King of Kings, full of Majesty, for He is worthy! Stand and support the cause of the Lord! For God has saved the lost and wiped away impurity from the earth. He has fought my battles and revealed my righteousness with His mighty hand."

My help comes from Yahweh, the Creator of heaven and earth, who holds everything together by His power. Who can compare to You, Lord? Is there anyone in heaven or on earth like You? You are pure and holy, and You do not tolerate anything unclean. You rule over all, and Your words bring life and truth. From the very beginning, You set Your plans in place, and nothing can change what You have decided. Even through hardships, You have drawn my heart toward You, and Your mark is upon me as a sign of Your favor.

You have given me the branches of the vine and the palms of righteousness. You have taken away my pride and replaced it with a deep respect for You. You have given me a heart that is forever cleansed. Because of this,

I will praise You always and give thanks among the nations. You have rescued me with a powerful salvation and shown kindness to David, Your chosen one, and his descendants forever.

As the song ended, I heard another voice from heaven, strong and clear, saying, "You are My son, My firstborn, My most cherished. Didn't I bring you across Shihor so that you would be My daily joy? But you rejected My gifts and mixed impurity with purity. That is why these things have come upon you. Still, among all living creatures, who is like you? Many have found protection in your shadow, and through your suffering, they have been healed. Think carefully about what is before you.

Because you have stayed true to the words of the shepherd all your life and remained in the Son without straying, this honor is now yours. You will be lifted up in glory and crowned with the splendor of the Lord."

I, Gad, son of Ahimelech, from the Jabez family of the tribe of Judah, was overwhelmed by this vision. My spirit shook within me, and I could not contain my awe. Then the one dressed in linen came down to me. His presence was calm but full of authority. He touched me and spoke, saying, "Write these words and seal them with the seal of truth, for Yahweh is My Name. By My Name, you will bless the whole house of Israel, for they are My chosen people, a nation of truth and promise.

You will continue your journey for a little while longer before you are peacefully gathered to your ancestors. But in the last days, you will see these things again—not as shadows or visions, but in their complete truth and reality. You will witness them with your own eyes, exactly as they were meant to be, in all their glory.

In that time, they will no longer be called Jacob but Israel, for no trace of sin will remain among them. They will belong fully to Yahweh, purified and set apart for His divine purpose. These words will bring renewal to you, filling your life and spirit with their truth and promise.

This will be a sign for you: when you enter the city, you will find My servant David reading these very words from the Book of the Covenant: 'Even when they are in the land of their enemies, I will not reject them or destroy them completely or break My covenant with them. For I am Yahweh, their God.'

You must tell David about the vision you have seen and the message you have received. When he hears your words and sees you, his heart will be filled with joy, for he will know that Yahweh has spoken and fulfilled His promise."

And so it happened that when I arrived at the house of David, the servant of God, I found him just as the man in linen had said. He was sitting and reading the words of the covenant with deep reverence and humility. I approached him and told him everything I had seen and the message I had been commanded to give.

When David heard my account, he lifted his voice to Yahweh and sang a song of love and worship: "I love You, Yahweh, my strength and my refuge." His words poured out with the deep trust of someone who knows that God's promises never fail.

Then David turned to me and said, "You are truly blessed before the Lord, for He has chosen to reveal His mysteries to you. How fortunate you are to witness His truth and carry His message."

I also lifted my voice in praise, saying, "Blessed are You, Yahweh, for You have not forgotten Your covenant with Your people. You are faithful, and Your word stands firm. Your promise remains unbroken, a sign of Your endless love and faithfulness." Hallelujah!

Thank You for Reading

Dear Reader,

We hope this timeless classic has sparked your imagination and enriched your literary journey. Now that you've turned the final page, we want to share a vision for the future of reading—one where every classic you've ever wanted to explore is at your fingertips, in a format that best suits your life.

We'd like to invite you to gain immediate, unlimited digital & audiobook access to hundreds of the most treasured literary classics ever written—along with the option to secure deluxe paperback, hardcover & box set editions at printing cost. Together, we can spark a new global literary renaissance alongside our small, independent publishing house called "The Library of Alexandria."

Thousands of years ago, the Library of Alexandria stood as a beacon of knowledge—until it was lost to history. We aim to reignite that spirit of preservation and discovery right now, in the modern age—only this time, it's accessible to all, in every language and every format.

Picture a world where every timeless classic, novel, poem, or philosophical treatise is not only available to read but also updated for today's readers—modernized, translated into any language or dialect, and ready to enjoy in any format you choose, whether that is in an eBook, audiobook, paperback, or deluxe hardcover & box set version a printing cost.

By joining our movement to rebuild the modern Library of Alexandria, you become part of an unprecedented mission to offer:

- **Unlimited Audiobook & eBook Access to the Greatest Classics of All Time**

    Instantly explore thousands of legendary works, from Plato and Shakespeare to Jane Austen and Leo Tolstoy. All are instantly ready to read or listen to, giving you a complete literary universe at your fingertips.

- **Paperback & Deluxe Editions at Printing Costs:**

    Purchase any title in a paperback, deluxe hardbound, or deluxe boxset edition at printing costs, shipped right to your doorstep. Curate your personal library of Alexandria with editions worthy of display—crafted to last, designed to captivate, and delivered straight to your door.

- **Modern translations for Contemporary Readers in all languages and dialects**

  Discover a vast selection of classics reimagined in clear, current language—no more struggling with outdated phrases or obscure references. Next to the original versions, we aim to offer translations in as many languages and dialects as possible.

  As we continue our translation efforts and add new languages, readers everywhere can connect with these works as if they were written today. By bridging linguistic divides, you're contributing to ensuring that these timeless stories become more meaningful, accessible, and inspiring for people across the globe.

- **Your Personal Library of Alexandria:**

  Over the months and years, you'll curate a unique physical archive of classics—each volume a testament to your taste, curiosity, and love of knowledge. It's not just about owning books—it's about curating a cultural legacy you'll cherish and pass down for generations to come.

- **Join a Global Literary Renaissance:**

  Your support fuels an ongoing mission: allowing us to reinvest in offering deluxe print editions (including special boxsets) at their true cost, broaden the range of available formats and translations, and extend the reach of these works to new audiences worldwide. By joining today, you're not just preserving a legacy of masterpieces; you set in motion a powerful wave of literary accessibility.

We are more than a publisher—we're a movement, and we can't do it alone. Your support lets us scale our mission, preserving and reimagining history's greatest works for tomorrow's readers.

Become a Torchbearer of knowledge.

Thank you for picking up this book and allowing us into your literary journey. As you turn the pages, know that you're part of something larger: a global effort to keep these stories alive, share their wisdom across borders and generations, and spark a true cultural revival for the modern era.

If this resonates with you—please consider taking the next step by visiting:

www.libraryofalexandria.com

With gratitude and a shared love of knowledge,

The Modern Library of Alexandria Team

Visit:

www.libraryofalexandria.com

Or scan the code below:

www.ingramcontent.com/pod-product-compliance
Lightning Source LLC
LaVergne TN
LVHW030632080426
835512LV00021B/3471